Grass Roots Poems

Thought provoking

Outrageous

Humorous

Controversial

Poetry about everyday life

By Robert Kemp

Grass Roots Poems

Copyright © Robert Kemp 2019

ISBN 13:978-1-9877-2469-1

Table of contents:

A Bugs World

With rubber gloves, apron and rather old hat,
I start to clean my dusty old flat,

By taking position upon my knees,
I spray the carpet for dust mites and fleas,

I bleach the toilet, sink and then the kitchen floor,
Trying to kill those germs that continue to spore,

I vacuum soft furnishings, like my carpet and suite,
Surely my efforts to kill them, have got those bugs beat?

I take out my rug and hang it out flat,
Then beat it insanely, just missing the cat,

I continue to clean the oven and fridge door,
This scrubbing and rubbing is making me sore,

Then with crevices probed and surfaces clean,
The rooms of my flat begin to gleam,

I take a few steps back to survey my good deed,
Only to be met with an itching feeling,
And soon I begin to bleed,

Were all my efforts totally in vain?
I'm starting to itch around my ankles again.

Allotment Alliance

Sex, ugh, he'd rather love the land,
Than spend the time to hold my hand,

The latest peas bring him to his knees,
It was the same last year and the year before,
His tending that patch is a real bore,

Once a year he displays his lot,
Which from what I've seen, is not a lot,

He loves to fertilise and spread his seed,
Then hoe around encroaching weed,

Next door's melons have taken his eye,
If the problem persists, I'll wave him good-bye,

Fungal problems, he's had quite a few,
Though with the right medication,
He's always pulled through,

From elongated cucumbers, to oversized marrows,
He spends most of his time at war with the sparrows,

From a tipped up turnip, to a worm riddled carrot,
He sits in his shed drinking best matured claret,

From bunions to onions and calluses galore,
If not tending his patch, he's sweeping the floor,

Take it from me though, if your blokes a grower,
Get him to turf his patch and buy him a mower.

Bluebell Wood

An endless woodland carpet,
Laid down among the trees,
Thousands of shimmering violet-blue flowers,
Helped on by a passing breeze,

Their sweet perfumed prevailing scent,
Invades the ancient forest floor,
Attracting animals to sniff the air,
Then sniff again for more,

Like Mother Nature's signal,
That spring's returned again,
These violet-blue bouquets of flowers,
Are washed with showery rain,

Like a mass gathering of trumpeters,
Awaiting the royal parade,
Slowly their colour less distinctive,
As daylight starts to fade.

Body Sculpture

Posing and pumping are the name of the game,
My weight lifting antics will send you insane,

I aim for a body that's massive but cut,
That's perfect in profile right down to one's foot,

With biceps and triceps pumped to the max,
My body is tanned and my hair is well waxed,

I've trained many months for this moment in time,
As I spread over oil that makes my skin shine,

I pose in the mirror and recheck my routine,
Did I really diet enough to be properly seen?

I start pumping each body part as best as I can,
Someone shouts in the distance it must be a fan?

I readjust my number so it rests above my thigh,
Suddenly a rush of adrenalin sends me onto a high,

I finish off with press-ups and small drink to quell my thirst,
My body feeling so pumped up, I'm ready to almost burst,

Then someone shouts across to me, "It's your turn to get on stage," it's time to start a new chapter in life, so now to turn the page,

I walk towards the curtains and push them out of the way,
I continue onto the podium, determined to make this my greatest day.

Capitalist Capitulation

Slowly one is consumed into a state of total despair,
With unemployment rising and no one out there to care,

The state is almost bankrupt and the banks have all closed
their doors, they say I'm over skilled and now I'm washing
floors,

The bailiffs called the other day to seize all that I own,
I've managed to call them off for now by taking out a loan,

Money that could not be found to help the sick and old, has
mysteriously materialised to stop a bank to fold,

Languishing on the edge of the abyss, the dreams I once had
slowly dissolve,

All I can do is live in hope that the world can adapt, and re-
evolve, the global fate of 2008.

Car-ma-sutra

The love of my life is made out of metal,
We're best on the move; I try not to settle,

Three times a week I wash this beauty of mine,
Using wax and a duster to bring out the shine,

It's full of electrics and alloys galore,
This car really shifts when my foot hits the floor,

From its leather clad seats to a wood filled dash,
It would break my heart if we had a crash,

The beefed up music gives a heart thumping sound,
So when I'm out cruising you'll know I'm around,

But this metallic marvel of mine often has me in tears,
When I think of the joy it's brought through the years,

But all good journeys must come to an end,
And a few months from now she'll be sold to a friend.

Cash from the Trash

I'm a dustman, don't rubbish my name,
Without out my services you'd go totally insane,

I collect your rubbish and take it away,
Allowing you to create more the following day,

You're throwing of trash, is my making of cash,

From a Chippendale chair, to a broken brolly,
I've even found a supermarket trolley,

I've always moved rubbish, it's part of my life,
From the bin in the street, to the in-law and wife,

I've been chased by dogs, even scratched with a syringe,
But at the end of the day; I'm not one to whinge,

From an engine block, to a trunk of a tree,
You've tried your best to rid it for free,

I've collected old beds,
Then sold them on to newlyweds,

My own three-piece was from the tip,
The matching curtains came from a skip,

The wheelie bin came from across the sea,
A great idea, making life easier for me,

Just remember this though; a wheelie bin is not a skip,
So please be careful what you tip.

Celluloid Psychopaths

There are two types of human being that walk the earth today,
The ones that use their mobiles in a safe and careful way,

The other types of humans are harder to be seen,
They hide their mobile phones beneath their window screens,

Risking life and limb to Facebook friends afar,
Updating social networks, while driving in their car,

These people know the risks, but do it all the same,
They really do put, the human race to shame,

Killing family members, or strangers in their path,
These crazy human beings are classed as psychopaths,

Mobiles cause distractions and much more should be done,
To rid these dangerous people, who flout the law for fun,

Self-driving cars would allow mobile use,
But until that day arrives, there's no real excuse,

Reading text messages, or talking on the phone,
Is not recommended while driving, so leave the phone alone!

Conniving Colleagues

I love my job; it's my colleagues I hate,
Telling my boss if I'm slightly late,

With fornication the name of the game,
These colleagues of mine will send me insane,

Bringing me down before a jobs even done,
This competition at work just isn't much fun,

Everyone wants to prove that they're better than me,
But I'm not their real competition, yet they fail to see,

Working together would send production much higher,
Than being a manipulative multiple liar,

So stand back for a minute and think what you've done,
We could all work together and make it more fun.

Curry Slurry

Bloody hell what a smell,
To have a curry and then poo like hell,

With my anus burning after this supper delight,
My food palate activated by an alcoholic night,

Why should food like this give my bowls such displeasure?
When all I was doing was drinking at leisure,

My stomachs in turmoil as the gas hits the air,
People wafting their noses with a displeasing stare,

A volcanic seismic event that will eventually blow,
As the contents of my stomach have nowhere to go,

Then there's a pause for a minute, followed by a strange
rumbling sound,
My curry is on the move again, a gastric outward bound,

This concoction of digested spices and herbs, mixed around
with fermented beer,
Is ejected with force to my behind and spread around my rear,

With bum cheeks clenched, there's no time to waste,
I shuffle to the toilet with an uneasy haste.

Daylight Slobbery

Life can be easy, why not visit and see,
Though I don't really like to mix socially,

Trust me; all you need are some cans and a big comfy chair,
Position the telly and focus your stare,

Remote viewing was a dream come true,
Only having to move to visit the loo,

With a mobile fridge and food by my side,
Spending most of the day with my legs spread out wide,

Two hundred channels and pay as you view,
Stuff going to pictures and joining a queue,

Though eventually, I will have to move to go to my bed,
Watching telly can be tiring,

Enough said.

Depression Expression

I'm feeling so lonely, depressed, sometimes totally insane,
A family member of mine, says I'm only to blame,

Friends I once knew are all out of my life,
The only person left is a disgruntled wife.

I sit many hours just staring at walls,
Just hoping and waiting, but nobody calls,

Watching clock hands speed on with my life,
With moaning and groaning from a once loving wife,

She seems so distant and does her own thing,
And lives at the bingo and has the odd fling,

Could doing the lottery feed me some hope?
Before it's too late and I'm unable to cope,

I've still got my health though; it's my mind that's all grey,
Hoping and waiting for a much brighter day.

Disco Dinosaur

From pubs to clubs, I've had my fill,
I've picked them up, was she on the pill?

I've been around the clock too many times to mention,
Twelve years from now I'll be on my pension,

I've propped up bars, and talked with stars,

From top notch suits, to well-groomed hair,
I've turned more heads than Fred Astaire,

But my designer clothes have all had their day,
So it's into the drawers and there they'll stay,

No more flirting about and staying out late,
Strutting the floor and laying the bait,

These years of partying have taken their toll,
It's time to grow up and alter my goal!

Dying Fly

I am a fly and it won't be long until I die,

Around twenty-eight days to mate, eat and fly,
So out from the pupa and into the sky,

I'll vomit on anything that looks a delight,
I can taste with my feet and mate in mid-flight,

I only mate once though, so can't be too picky,
And my favourite food is usually quite sticky,

With claws and pads upon my feet,
Allowing me to land, rest, and eat,

Transporting germs to food on display,
So if I'm flying around, just hide it away,

I could have just feasted upon horse poo,
Then landed and transported it right onto you,

Decaying matter is what I seek,
From domestic waste, to a toilet leak,

Even rotting corpses from different type mammals,
From the smallest field mouse to the largest hump camels,

From maggots to flies in less than two weeks,
The hot summer days are what a fly seeks,

We're only regenerating the left over waste,
So let the flies lay their eggs and fly around in haste.

14

Feline Friend

Our cat sits majestically on the window sill,
Very alert and ready to kill,

Then suddenly he starts to heave, he's going to be sick,
For a furball beckons, so you have to be quick,

I scoop him up quickly and run to the door,
But if I'm slightly too late, he'll furball my floor,

He's sharpened his claws on my draylon settee,
Climbed up the curtains and sprayed on my knee,

Vet and food bills have cost me a packet,
And his fighting and crying cause a terrible racket,

He's also drawn blood, when teased or in shock,
And will lose total control, if you throw him a sock,

But all this is worth it in the end,
Because he'll never deceive me,

My little feline friend.

Gauntlet of the Ghetto

Afraid to leave my house at night,
Those drunken louts they start to fight,

I've been spat at and robbed,
I've sobbed, many times I've sobbed,

Prostitution and drugs are rife,
Was I only born to live this life?

They've turned my life into a hell,
If I had the right, I'd try to sell,

What's wrong with the youth today?
 Scared to work, don't need the pay,

Gambling, drinking and hooked on coke,
They ruin the lives of us decent folk,

My kids have all flown and I'm on my own,
But I do my best and rarely moan,

The future looks bleak, for the things that I seek.

Global Warming

Our earth struggles against climate change,
Because what we find we re-arrange,

Turning wood to ash,
Using coal from the soil,
Makes this earth want to boil,

As Pollutants rise into our skies,
Will we ever realise?

To keep this Eden of ours so fine,
We must learn to re-align,

Our ways must change,
Or else we'll die,

Help save the planet,
Or say good-bye!

Grave Times Ahead

Many corpses lay beneath my feet,
This resting place is not the street,

But a holy place where the dead can lay,
Often made of granite, marble, stone or clay,

A wooden box sent deep below,
The time did come for them to go,

They lay in silence in their many rows,
The only noise made by the crows,

Old weathered wreathes adorn these plots,
With colour gone, many long forgot,

These lifeless shells from a previous life,
With many lying with a once loved wife,

If you seek a place of solitude,
Then this is the place for you,

A time to think of the good times gone,
Of the loved ones you once knew,

But freshly dug holes await the dead,
The next hole could be yours instead,

So watch your next step,
And live life to the full,

Before the grim reaper begins his new cull!

Humanoid or Paranoid

Artificial intelligence is knocking at our door, with super computer quantum physics becoming quite a bore,

Will future robotic androids help us to do our chores? They make them sound so capable, but can they wash my floors?

A redundant male because of this, would remove my loving spouse, my husband does all the jobs needed around the house,

Suddenly I feel full of glee; it could be used in a positive way, to replace my husband for a brand new model, with a robot that can work all day,

It would only talk if I asked it to and could service my intimate needs, only needing oil and an electric point and wouldn't need to feed,

My nagging hubby would be a thing of the past; these robots could save the day, these electronic manoeuvrable walking machines would allow me to have the last say.

K-9 Capers

I have a dog that I love to walk,
We often pass others, who love to talk,

It must be the best socializing tool around,
As I met my wife as she walked her hound,

Free exercise is also included,
But the worse things of all must not be eluded,

The downside to my beautiful mutt,
Is when he lowers his oversized butt,

With legs slightly parted and a smell in the air,
He leaves a large load, leaving people to stare,

This steaming monstrosity is now in my care,
Which I find quite revolting and very unfair,

Trying to scoop softies without the right tools,
Can lead the dog owners to breaking the rules,

I could do a runner, but I'd be guilty as sin,
Not to put this creation wrapped up in a bin,

Why can't dogs wear some kind of nappy?
Keeping me and Joe public much more happy.

Kipper Stripper

As I prepare myself with oil,
The atmosphere starts to boil,

While adjusting my thong,
They start playing my song,

It's time to go on and do the show,
I'm all dressed up and ready to go,

As I enter the stage there's a roar from the crowd,
A number of girls start shouting out loud,

I partly remove some clothing,
And give them a wink and a stare,
To make them think that I'm interested,
When honestly, I don't really care,

I wiggle my body and mime to the song,
The sweat and the oil make a terrible pong,

I let a girl peek at what I've got,
Which I can tell you now is quite a lot,

The audience whipped themselves into a frenzy,
And soon they shout out for more,
So I completely strip, do an athletic flip,
And strut around the floor,

I can't believe I'm paid, to do something I enjoy,
Those girls down there would love a date,
And use me as their toy,

Eventually the show comes to an end,
I pick up my clothes with an undignified bend,

With a flash of my bum, I wave to the crowd,
I exit the stage and on to collect my wage.

Laptop Lunatic

She's always on her laptop,
Or texting on her phone,
And even though I married her,
It's like being home alone,

Her offspring prance in front of her,
With an attention seeking display,
They want some love from a mother,
That hurries them away,

"I'll just be a minute,"
She shouts out once again,
This pc obsessive woman,
Is becoming quite a pain,

Maybe I should text her,
Or ring her on her phone,
At least I'll get an answer,
Even though we're both at home!

Legalised Robbery

Loans are made easy with limitless cash,
All you do is have to ask,

The more you borrow the bigger the debt,
Longer to pay, longer to fret,

Some loan sharks here will suck you dry,
Control your life and make you cry,

From shark to shark life spirals out of control,
You lose your health; you've sold your soul,

From a long term debtor, to a nasty written letter,
We'll seize your goods, maybe take the car,
You'll pay us now, you won't get far,

A cycle of total despair, I'm going absolutely nowhere,
Smothered by loans, pestered by phones,

A bailiff calls saying, "If you cannot pay you shouldn't borrow,"
So I slam the door, I'll pay tomorrow,

So think long and deep, you people of wealth,
Enjoy your life; I'll toast your health!

Miracle of Life

Life begins with sudden light,
A burst of breath,
Then starts the fight,

A thirst for knowledge is now in flow,
As each day passes,
I start to grow,

But is this it?
Or is there more?
A smiling face does reassure,

I try to stand,
But my legs are weak,
A helping hand is what I seek,

I start to tire,
The things I've seen,
It makes me want to start to scream,

If this is life,
I want some more,
The futures mine,

God bless us all!

My Dear Mother

My mother, she stresses and toils each day,
She has no time for rest or play,

Her workload is large and so is her heart,
I dread the day when we have to part,

She's kind, thoughtful and always to hand,
If I have a problem she'll understand,

We take our mothers for granted too much,
So spare a few thoughts,
I'm sure she'll be touched.

My Wife, My Life

My wife, my buddy, my friend close to me,
If I have a problem she'll have the key,

She's softly spoken, like her skin is to touch,
I often do tell her I love her so much,

We're a couple, an item, a marriage decree,
I'll walk her in hand for others to see,

My wife, my life, a reason to live,
The pleasure is mine; I'm learning to give,

Life can be hard for others I know,
But for this moment in time, ours is beginning to grow.

Neighbourly Love

I wake up in the morning,
Then I wash, dress and eat,
I kiss my wife upon the face,
And head out for the street,

But as I leave my humble home,
My neighbour does the same,
So should I shout good morning?
Or ignore him once again,

I used to say good morning first,
But nothing was said back,
To judge the mood of this bloody fool,
Is becoming quite a knack,

The times he's looked straight through me,
As though I'm an empty space,
With a total look of ignorance,
Spread across his vacant face,

Do you really hate me that much?
To pretend that I'm not there,
Or are you a part of the human race,
That doesn't really care?

Nipple Tipple

My darling baby cries, with swollen eyes,
She needs her mother, with clean warm cover,

Her mother uncovers her food laden breast,
With head caressed, she feeds with zest,

Suddenly her cries subside,
But with eyes still open wide,

Just when it looks as though she's had her fill,
With nipple slightly sore, she cries for even more,

Eventually this food on tap,
Makes her feel quite sleepy, she'll want to nap,

This action can never be classed as being crude,
After all it's only baby food,

This elixir of life,
Produced by my wife.

Obliteration Altercation

Thermal nuclear annihilation is knocking at our door,
With the Russians and North Koreans now threatening us with war,

A radioactive waste land is what will be left behind,
With a nuclear winter landscape the victors will only find,

They say we need these missiles to destroy the enemy first,
A no win situation, with mankind so cruelly cursed,

With total disunity growing, the end of the world is nigh,
When we see those mushroom clouds, high up in a crimson sky,

Sun scorched deep earth craters, will be spread across our land, with radioactive fallout, the two go hand in hand,

Our vegetation will wither and the seas become dark and cold,
As the ozone loss and deadly frosts begin to take their hold,

The hemisphere and stratosphere will be choked with dust and smoke, blocking out the warm sun's rays and dashing any hope,

The human race will cease to be, if we carry along this road,
So let's address our problems now, before the seeds are sowed.

One Day

One day I'm going to be a millionaire,
Without a worry or a care,

I'll control my life and steer it through,
The happy go fella that I once knew,

With a custom limo and a fancy boat,
And a modern day castle with an all-around moat,

Own land as far as the eye can see,
And knowing it all belongs to me,

I'll walk into shops that were just dreams before.
And buy clothes and hats and labels galore,

Designer clothes with lots of jewels,
With me making up all the rules,

A wheelie bin full of champagne bottles,
And beefed up cars with go fast throttles,

With parties plenty and hobbies galore,
My time well spent, will be lost no more,

I'll travel the world from end to end,
And meet many people and maybe a friend,

Waking in the mornings without using alarms,
Being full of composure, happy and calm,

Beautiful women that turned me away,
Will give me their numbers and ask me to stay,

I'd eat at posh restaurants and dance until dawn,
Then sleep off my partying on a manicured lawn,

I've the same chance as any, in having this fun,
When my numbers come up, I'll know it's begun.

Plane Crazy

To me, flying is like dying, but to travel is my job,
So I suffer in silence and try not to sob,

I check in my cases and depart from the lounge,
Then walk to the plane, I must be insane,

This fuel filled coffin is ready to go,
With its engines fired up and its lights all aglow,

I clamber up the stairs to stewards waiting at the top,
I'm greeted with smiles, then led down the aisle,

I eventually become seated and strap myself in,
A few moments later there's a terrible din,

We speed down the runway with my heart in my mouth,
We're heading out north, but my stomach's gone south,

Suddenly we become airborne; I'm now in their hands,
I think of my will and my funeral plans,

A baby starts crying, someone coughs in my ear,
The person in front starts downing a beer,

Three hundred farts I'll swallow today,
Plus coughing, wheezing, belching and sneezing,

The remain seated sign leaves my bladder ready to burst,
My mouth is so dry and I'm dying of thirst,

Nine hours later my bum feels so sore,
This position on my body can't take anymore,

Suddenly the plane shudders and we look in dismay,
Has time caught us up, is this our last day?

Eventually we land, I sigh with relief,
Take a few deep breaths and unload my grief.

Political Leeches

Politicians, they make me sick,
You vote them in; it's all a trick,

Increase your tax, decrease your wealth,
Stress you out and harm your health,

The NHS, roads and rail,
Are in collapse and bound to fail,

They promise the earth, but strip you bare,
But they're alright; they don't need to care,

If you're on a pension, you've had your lot,
You've fought through wars, they've long forgot,

Don't invite one around for tea,
They'll take your wife and pinch the key,

Promises, predictions, they know it all,
They want your vote; they've got the gall,

Rid this world of political strife,
Learn to take orders from no one,
But your wife!

Power to the People

Wind turbines, solar panels and maybe the sea,
Seem much safer options of power to me,

Nuclear waste is with us for years,
Contamination is what everyone fears,

Radiation can cause problems and defects at birth,
Blown in by the wind and mixed with the earth,

If we treasure this life upon this land,
Nuclear power will have to be banned,

There's no going back, once the damage has been done,
You'll have to move house, you'll be on the run,

For to stay will mean death or suffering for sure,
So stand and be counted, then worry no more.

Prevailing Poverty

Life is hard, a real struggle,
Trying to live in this house of rubble,

With good times few and far between,
I find it hard to live the dream,

The stench of damp, it fills the air,
I've had three kids, all now in care,

Bronchitis, pneumonia, I've had the lot,
If there's a God, he's lost the plot,

Kids clunk around in their mothers shoes,
She doesn't care; she's on the booze,

Fighting, stealing, drugs and sex,
It's a world away from Posh and Becks,

I live in dreams to travel afar,
But all I've got is a burnt out car,

Alone and afraid of the long cold night,
If people care, they're out of sight,

I try to make do with what I've got,
Which as you can see is not a lot.

Reps to Riches

With a dry-cleaned suit and a well styled tie,
I'm a top notch rep, who's ready to fly,

Outgoing, dynamic, I dream to aspire,
To win rep of the year, or to go even higher,

From grid locked motorways, to six feet of snow,
If you've made an appointment I won't let it go,

Fresh and frozen is what I sell,
I do my job and do it well,

Deadlines to meet and quotas to beat,
I'm a sales representative, who's rushed off their feet,

Desk bound pen pushers can keep their lot,
There's a world out there they've long forgot,

Every day is different, like the people that I meet,
Whether it's a cold winter's morning, or in the midsummers
heat.

Road Rage

I'm a mild mannered man,
Don't touch the booze,
Moderately dressed,
With well-polished shoes,

But when I get into my car,
I don't have to travel very far,
There's a change in me that's so profound,
I want to fight anyone that's around,

They drive too slowly,
They're up my rear,
From a total Neanderthal,
To the little old dear,

From the twenty mile an hour cruiser,
To the over the limit boozer,
If they don't watch their step,
They'll end up with a bruiser,

Oblivious to other drivers,
They don't know what they've done,
Creating total chaos,
As deadly as a gun,

Altercations, I've had quite a few,
So just be careful when you're on the road again,
The next one could be you.

Sanctuary of Solitude

A morbid silence encompasses these heavenly plots before me. The morning mist seems to linger much longer around these sacred burial grounds, than it does in neighbouring fields,

A multitude of timeworn monuments in quality stone, set into regimental rows, trying their best to fight off the gravitational weight, which will eventually bring them down,

A conveyor belt of brambles and tree roots, gradually invading and smothering these weathered tombstones, already cracked and worn by time immemorial,

This is not only a place for Mother Nature to slowly absorb the rotting carcases of mankind, but is also a time for her to be repatriated with her children, that once walked upon her Gardens of Eden,

This a sacred place, where sordid souls can seek eternal peace. Where they have been stripped of their human form and have now become mere ghosts of the past,

But as I scour this area of the ancient dead, I notice a strange sense of calm, as though time itself has been stopped in its tracks. Allowing time for one to reflect on one's own life and the past lives of others,

This is the human race, on its relentless journey of some kind of metamorphosis, from the cradle to the grave and beyond.

School of Crime

This life of mine, this life of crime,
I rob to live and not to give,

Your hard earned labours,
Are my fruits yet to pick,
The way I earn my living,
Will often make you sick,

House, shop, bike, or car,
If it's not locked I won't be far,
I'm mean; I'm keen and hard to catch,
Don't leave that door upon a latch,

I've tried to work; it's not for me,
9 to 5 then have your tea,
I'll work at night and sleep all day,
I call the shots to earn my pay,

The adrenalin rush sends me on a high,
If I am caught I know I'll fry,
Jo public likes to buy my goods old or new,
The biggest criminal out there is you!

Silver Threads

My hair is grey,
My teeth are yellow,
It's hard to hear, you'll have to bellow,

My bones, they creak,
My nails are brown,
My wrinkles deep, I do so frown,

I'm shrinking fast,
I feel so cold,
I've lost some hair,
I'm almost bald,

Road map veins adorn my legs,
I shuffle around on two thin pegs,

My skins so dry,
And muscles weak,
A long nice rest is what I seek,

Just remember this though,
Without us old folk you wouldn't be here,
So give me your hand and help an old dear.

Soldiers of Freedom

I bow my head to the millions of dead,
To the brave heroic stories that will never be read,

Many suffered in silence too proud to complain,
These soldiers of freedom marched on through the rain,

Longing to see their loved ones, many miles from home,
A soldier's life could feel empty and very alone,

Heroic in battle, but wary of war, they would help protect
colleagues, who belonged to their core,

With friendships forged, then suddenly lost,
This great mental torture would have a great cost,

They didn't do it for money, status, or greed,
But were called by their country to fulfil a need,

With a bloodied body and a sweaty brow,
They did us proud, only god knows how,

So you younger people do spare them a thought, freedoms
well kept, but freedoms hard fought.

Stone Sanctuary

This quaint and tranquil cottage, with an awe inspiring view,
Doth rest the weary traveller, as they are passing through,

A history time locked capsule, of stone and slate in grey,
Uneven weathered moss clad walls, do face another day,

If only ghosts locked within these walls, could talk of ancestral
past and tell you of the good times gone and how long they
did last,

A stone created habitat, which doth stand the test of time,
And surely here deserves some words, created in a rhyme.

Stormy Seas

Like a rabid dog, the sea foams the shore,
Rolling back and forth for ever-more,

I've seen the sea almost mountain high,
This usually happens with darkened sky,

The sea's at best with a storm in flow,
With awesome power and crushing blow,

Some like the peace of a placid lake,
That's not for me, for pity's sake,

A clap of thunder, a flash of light,
This ocean here is full of fight,

Never under-estimate this beauty of a beast,
Or you'll become its latest feast!

Stud Work

I'm cool, sexy and a pleasure to see,
If you fancy a taste, I'll lend you my key,

With round pert buttocks and a well filled crotch,
If you treat me just right, I'll allow you to touch,

I've a full head of hair and a sly sexy stare,
One night spent with me and you won't have a care,

I'll tease you and please you, till the night turns to day,
Then you'll be left broken hearted, as you beg me to stay,

But it's time to move on, no ties for me please,
Into your life, then out like the breeze.

Sweat Shop Lover

Fourteen hours I can work each day,
The work is hard for such small pay,

The dust, the dirt, the deep driven grime,
Is a reason not to want to work, such a terrible crime?

I do all this to pay my bills,
The strain of work it often kills,

With pleasures few and far between,
I often dream of pastures green,

My problems continue when I return home at night,
With my body drained, I'm ready to give up the fight,

The wife at home is full of beans,
She says, "let's make love," but it's not as easy as it seems,

For I am worn out and ready for my bed,
So I just look towards my darling and pretend to nod my head,

But I know and she knows, that when I hit the sack,
She'd need a resuscitation unit to try and bring me back.

The Fiery Hearth

I have an open fire,
With a beautiful surround,
The pleasure this fire gives me,
Is really so profound,

I sweep out all the ashes,
And load it up with coal,
The warming feeling you'll get from this,
Will really lift your soul,

I start by lighting tinder,
And watch the fire unfold,
There's nothing out there better,
For keeping out the cold,

Soon the fire is roaring,
And the room is warm as toast,
Dancing shadows from the flames,
Create a fiery ghost,

But slowly the yellow flames turn to orange,
And the embers can be seen,
It starts to radiate volcanic colours,
Creating an hypnotic gleam,

I give the fire a hurried poke,
To rekindle the dying flames,
The people who visit me while the fires alight,
Are happy that they came,

I cannot wait until tomorrow comes,
When I can light it once again!

The Medical Detective

Hi, I'm your local GP,
A multitude of people I often do see,

You have three to five minutes to tell me your lot,
From a compound fracture to a suspected clot,

From palpitations to lacerations,
Internal inspections to runny infections,

Haemorrhoids to herpes,
Or maybe the tetanus jab,
And if you really need it a total rehab,

You've had me in stitches, if you pardon the pun,
From self-inflicted knife wounds,
To a zit infested bum,

Though I'll try my best to get you through,
Let's hope it's not terminal and it's only the flu.

The Secret Garden Beauty

You're like that perfect flower,
Locked away from prying eyes,
Never to be gazed upon,
Except by bees and butterflies,

Never to be loved or walked along,
Or serenaded with a loving song,
Never to be seen hand in hand,
Along golden beaches of soft exotic sand,

Like a veiled wedding beauty that no one ever sees,
Hidden like Sleeping Beauty, within a wall of trees,
I don't know why this happened to person such as you,
But I know by faded photos that this story was very true.

To Bee, or not to Bee

I'm the humble bumble bee,
There are millions more around like me,

We can live in the trees, or under the ground,
With my black and yellow stripes you'll know I'm around,

I come and go from our self-built hive,
But I don't mess around; I've no time to skive,

I fly around the flowers and buzz around the trees,
Making flying seem so easy, to me it's just a breeze,

Always searching for the perfect bouquet,
Hoping for a warm and sunny dry day,

I'm a gravity-defying bundle of fluff,
Covering myself like a powder puff,

Gathering nectar to add to our store,
Soon with legs laden, I can't take anymore,
So I hurry to the nest and crawl to its core,

Here lies the queen in the heart of our home,
Producing more workers to tend to her throne,

Patching and mending our honeycomb palace,
Feeding our queen from our honey tipped chalice,

Predators are many and we'll put up a fight,
Using our stings on the enemy in sight,

With my vivid stripes a warning to others,
That if I am attacked I've got hundreds of brothers,

Pesticides and farming are also a worry,
So to save us good bees you will have to hurry.

Traffic Trauma

The car, the lorry, motorbike on two wheels,
We need the transport everyone feels,

But I'm not too sure, as I breathe in their smoke,
Because as traffic grows, we start to choke,

The speed, the noise, in the fast lane we live,
But pollutants will grow and we'll have to give,

I like to walk and take in the view,
This might sound boring, to the many or the few,

Populations grow and so do the cars,
Maybe it would be better if I moved out to Mars,

They eat up the green belt and cover it with tar,
They say we must do it for the sake of the car,

They're noisy, smelly and can kill in a flash,
This rushing around will end in a crash,

So do as I do and throw down your keys,
Leave the car at home and exercise those knees.

Travel Mania

With a back pack, boots and my camouflage hat,
I check all my tickets and lock up my flat,

I'll be gone for a while, from this simple abode,
My journeys in motion, I'll now hit the road,

I've travelled the world and seen many things,
From Asia, the Pacific, to the Valley of the Kings,

From desert to jungle, mountains and snow,
I've kayaked great rivers to follow their flow,

By walking, donkey, camel or horse,
Some modes of transport that I've used on my course,

I've trekked many trails and walked thousands of miles,
Passing through long mountain ranges, to simple farm stiles,

You've only got one life, so live it to the full,
With my last dying breath, I'll know mine was never dull.

Trolley Trauma

I open my kitchen cupboards,
To find them almost bare,
I think I'll have to go shopping,
And within ten minutes I'm there,

It's early in the morning,
With hardly a soul in sight,
So I have no trouble parking,
That I used to get at night,

I gather my re-usable bags together,
And walk into the store,
I grab a trolley and pull it hard,
But end up on the floor,

My trolleys tangled with the one in front,
I can't free it from the others,
Suddenly my face turns red,
And I'm filled with dread,
As I'm helped by two expectant mothers,

I swiftly leave this embarrassing scene,
Only to find out to my dismay,
That the wheel of this trolley is broken,
As I'm forced in the opposite way,

I continue my journey as best I can,
And start filling my cart with food,
Suddenly I'm rammed in the rear,
By a little old dear,
Who mutters out something quite rude,

"The alley's too narrow,
And you are much wider,"
This lady continues to say,

(Cont'd)

51

So I move over briskly,
And let her pass by me,
To quickly get her out of the way,

My trolley continues to have a mind of its own,
As I rush through the alleys,
With this basket of chrome,

But soon the trolley is filled to the top,
I aim for a checkout,
And soon leave the shop,

The car park's almost empty,
Yet my car seems surrounded,
Why people want to park so close,
Leaves me totally dumbfounded,

Is all this trouble worth it in the end?
Next time I'll go online,
And just press send.

United We Stand

With an open heart,
And open hand,
Unite together,
Create a stand,

Shoulder to shoulder,
We'll see it through,
Brothers and sisters,
By your side with you,

Together as one,
We know no bounds,
It's not as crazy as it sounds,

Give hurt and evil a great big shove,
And replace this menace with total love.

Vindictive Vendor

My house is on the market,
They said it would take a while,
The agent looks at my portfolio,
And then begins to smile,

"I've got you lots of viewings,
They're waiting to be shown,
I'll let you know very soon by email or phone,"

But it's been on the market for nearly a year,
And when I do a viewing it's never very clear,

When they come to view my house,
They never come on time,
Always wanting to leave their shoes on,
Just working in the grime,

The times I've shown people around,
And tried to judge their mood,
Don't they like my décor?
But refrain from being rude,

The agent said reduce your price,
As this would seal a deal,
But the agent doesn't understand,
Just how I really feel,

Do they want to buy my house?
Or are they here to dwell,
Upon a house they can't afford,
A vendor's trying to sell.

<u>We</u>

We live, we say goodbye and then we die,
We hope to make a transition to the heavenly sky,

We hoped to have lived a fulfilling life,
And to have partnered happily with a loving husband or wife,

We know our actions will be set for ever in time,
And though the future has ceased to be, the past will always
be mine,

We hope to experience feelings that no other creatures can,
With love and hope at the top of the list, of many woman or
man.

What a Dank Dull Day

What a dank dull day,

When the primary colours seem to be made up of grey,
Depressingly consuming as the dark clouds are looming,

What a dank dull day,

When a multitude of colours seem to be lacking the scene,
Then the flora coloured pallet of summer has been,

What a dank dull day,

With damp moisture filling the air,
Cold and unpleasant and feeling of despair,

What a dank dull day,

When a wet sodden surface seems to cover the land,
As though God had wiped his brow with the back of his hand,

What a dank dull day,

Like a semi-night time presence, the day is unable to shed,
Maybe tomorrow will bring a better day instead?

Printed in Great Britain
by Amazon